John Davis Washburn

Address Delivered, July 4, 1876, at Lancaster, Massachusetts

John Davis Washburn

Address Delivered, July 4, 1876, at Lancaster, Massachusetts

ISBN/EAN: 9783744735476

Printed in Europe, USA, Canada, Australia, Japan

Cover: Foto ©ninafisch / pixelio.de

More available books at **www.hansebooks.com**

ADDRESS,

DELIVERED JULY 4, 1876,

AT

LANCASTER, MASSACHUSETTS,

BY REQUEST OF THE CITIZENS.

———————

BY

JOHN D. WASHBURN,

A FORMER RESIDENT OF THE TOWN.

———————

LANCASTER:

1876.

WORCESTER:

PRESS OF CHAS. HAMILTON.

1876.

PREFATORY NOTE.

At a legal meeting of the Voters of Lancaster, held April 3d, 1876, on motion of the Rev. A. P. Marvin, it was voted :—

"To refer the subject of the delivery and publication of a Centennial Address on the 4th of July next, to a Committee of five, and that the sum of $150 be appropriated for the same."

Elected as said Committee :—

Rev. A. P. Marvin,   Rev. G. M. Bartol,
Chas. T. Fletcher,   G. F. Chandler.
Henry S. Nourse.

This Committee was subsequently organized by the election of Mr. Bartol as Chairman, and of Mr. Nourse as Secretary and Treasurer. On motion of Mr. Marvin, Col. John D. Washburn was invited to deliver the address.

EXERCISES.

The following exercises were held in the Meeting-House of the First Parish; beginning precisely at Ten o'clock A. M.:—

ORGAN VOLUNTARY.

MY COUNTRY, 'TIS OF THEE.

(America.)

My country, 'tis of thee,
Sweet land of liberty,
    Of thee I sing;
Land where my fathers died,
Land of the pilgrims' pride,
From every mountain side
    Let freedom ring.

My native country, thee—
Land of the noble free—
    Thy name—I love;
I love thy rocks and rills,
Thy woods and templed hills,
My heart with rapture thrills
    Like that above.

Let music swell the breeze,
And ring from all the trees
    Sweet freedom's song;
Let mortal tongues awake;
Let all that breathe partake;
Let rocks their silence break,—
    The sound prolong.

Our fathers' God, to thee,
Author of liberty,
    To thee we sing;
Long may our land be bright
With freedom's holy light;
Protect us by thy might,
    Great God, our King.

6

PRAYER,

By Rev. Benjamin Whittemore, D. D.

HYMN,

By Benjamin B. Whittemore.

Almighty God, whose gracious hand
Has long sustained our favored land,
Thy people, now, in hymns of praise
Their grateful hearts and voices raise,
And for thy blessing humbly pray
To crown the glory of this day.

Thy sovereign power o'er all the earth
Attends the nations in their birth—
Thy wisdom giving each, aright,
Its meed of strength—its needed light,
All moving by Thy wond'rous plan,
To serve the final good of man.

Thy guiding hand our fathers knew,
Their faith was strong—their courage true,
With trust in Thee they fearless spoke
The words that stern oppression broke,
While Liberty, 'mid storm and strife,
Led forth a *nation* into life.

That nation with resistless tread
Forth on its mission boldly sped,
Though freedom's direst foes assailed,
Its loyal heart has never quailed,
And, in this proud centennial year.
It meets the world without a peer.

Lord, we behold our Father-land—
Its borders wide—its beauty grand—
While every plain and mountain crest
With freedom's signet seems impress'd,
And o'er its wide domain we see
A country blest, a people free.

And shall not this dear heritage
Our deep solicitude engage?
Lord, for our country may we live—
Help us devoted hearts to give,
That still her destiny may be
To bless mankind—to honor Thee.

READING OF DECLARATION OF INDEPENDENCE,

By Henry S. Nourse.

ODE,

By Mrs. Julia A. Fletcher Carney.*

One hundred years ago, our sires
  Unfurled the starry banner,
And lighting Freedom's signal fires
Even from their own funereal pyres,
  Shouted in glad Hosanna!
Old Massachusetts led the way!
  Her pine tree flag unfurling
Wherever,—on the battle day,—
Thickest and darkest o'er the fray,
  The smoke of death was curling.

The snowy flag beside the blue
  Still said, "Appeal to Heaven!"
Dark and yet darker grew its hue,
As mid the battle smoke it flew
  Till victory was given.
God of our sires, Thou still art here!
  We still, to Thee appealing,
Ask that this proud Centennial year
May leave us nobler, purer, freer
  From foes around us stealing.

Save, we beseech! Our nation's heart
  A myriad foes doth cherish!
Low men in places high have part,
A selfish greed doth fill each mart,
  Help! lest our country perish!
In olden time, against one foe
  Forth went our snowy banner;
Our newer flag, to-day doth know
No foeman for its mailed arm's blow,
  Yet still we cry, Hosanna!

---

* Extract from letter of Mrs. Carney; "It will be known to most of the older ones assembled, that in the early part of our Revolutionary War, our privateers all carried the *old* flag of Massachusetts. The field was of white,—in the centre a green pine tree;—the motto, 'Appeal to Heaven.' The star-spangled banner was not adopted till June 14th, 1776, and still the Massachusetts State flag was used with it.

The Hebrew meaning of Hosanna, 'Save, we beseech,' may interest the Sunday School children.

Of course, the present flag of our dear native State, with its mailed arm ready for a foe, yet its motto of peace, is familiar to all."

ORATION,

By John D. Washburn.

PSALM 44,

(Version of Tate & Brady.)

O Lord, our fathers oft have told,
  In our attentive ears,
Thy wonders in their days performed,
  And in more ancient years.

'Twas not their courage, nor their sword,
  To them salvation gave;
'Twas not their number nor their strength,
  That did their country save :

But Thy right hand,—Thy powerful arm,—
  Whose succor they implored;
Thy providence protected them,
  Who Thy great name adored.

To Thee the glory we'll ascribe,
  From whom salvation came;
In God, our shield, we will rejoice,
  And ever bless Thy name.

BENEDICTION,

By Rev. A. P. Marvin.

In further pursuance of their instructions, the Committee now publish the Address.

ADDRESS.

An accomplished and eloquent orator, in a commemorative address delivered some years ago in a neighboring State, spoke of the early days of this country as the " Age of Homespun ; " yet to it he attributed, by way of contrast to our own, most of the characteristics of a golden age. The address was graceful and charming, yet it may be doubted whether the pictures of the life of our fathers were not too highly colored, and whether the inferences which would naturally be drawn from what was said, are not, relatively, too unfavorable to the present day.

For was the age of homespun and the pillion the golden age of America ? Are we degenerate sons of nobler sires, as we gather to-day to commemorate and thank Heaven for the lives and labors and sacrifices of those who first made their abiding place in this Commonwealth, fugitives from a tyranny which sought to fetter the conscience and bind the soul in bonds of iron, of those also who,

2

in sacrifice and self devotion a hundred years ago laid the foundations of this Republic, then strong only in hope and the possibilities of the future, now imperial among the powers of the earth ? Is not the present as truly the golden age, bright with the acquisitions of the century just drawn to its close, the age of free thought and free men, of intellectual activity, of universal education, of religious equality, of scientific attainment, of the steamship, the railway and "the thoughts that shake mankind ?" Do we not most truly honor the fathers when we claim honor for their sons as a worthy race of descendants which, on the whole, has illustrated in its career the influence of their transmitted quality, which, on the whole, has even improved on the standard they set up, and which, though not maintaining every one of their signal virtues in the conspicuous degree they themselves did, has yet, in the main, preserved those and combined them with other good of which the Fathers dreamed not ? Is it wise, even in these days of commemoration, to magnify too much their merit in depreciation of our own? Honest, conservative, desponding minds there are to-day, which dwell persistently and painfully on the virtues of the Fathers, excluding all contemplation of their errors, and sighing over the decline of the virtues to-day, contrasting our failures with their attainments, ignoring alike their

short-comings and our peculiar and distinctive excellence. Sighs for the domestic purity of times
gone by, sighs for the simplicity of the Fathers,
sighs for the days when, in our country, political
corruption was unknown. Shut your eyes and
listen, and you will hear them breathed somewhere
even to-day. And so are the Fathers glorified and
the children shamed, and by the children's shame
are the Fathers glorified. Not so would I exalt the
founders of these Colonies and this Republic, rather
show forth their true glory by vindicating the claim
of their sons to legitimacy and honor.

Yet our disposition in this regard was theirs also.
In their day, not a few of them mourned their own
degeneracy, and deplored the existence among them
of evils as grave as those over which a portion of
our community sighs to-day. It is not the characteristic of the present age above all others, to
look back to the past for golden days. It is the
common propensity of every age. Hesiod, early
poet of Greece, but spoke the voice of his contem-
poraries when he said that men must look into a
vague and remote antiquity for the times when purity
and faith prevailed on the earth. Ovid, among the
Romans, describes the simplicity and virtues of the
remote golden age in his musical verse. The loftier
strains of Virgil repeat the same refrain, and
Tibullus echoes the sweet and melancholy tone.

But a few years later, the successors of these looked back to them with longings unutterable. They became the representatives of the golden age of morals, hardly less than of letters, and their days seemed as bright and guileless as had to them the days of Saturn. Christianity came, lighting up the dark places of earth with mild diffusive ray ; yet it was long before men ceased to look back to the Greek philosophy as of a loftier and purer type: nay, some have not wholly ceased to even now. I pass over illustrations of similar disposition from the writers of English literature, but remark that in the time of our revolution many good men mourned over the decay of virtue since the early colonial days, just as now, in the midst (grant it) of striking instances of personal and political unfaithfulness, we recur to the days of the Revolution as our golden age.

To say that this disposition is natural is but commonplace. We have its foundation in the character and distinctive quality of every succeeding past and present. As years elapse individuality lessens. It is the individual always withering and the world always more and more. By consequence, the patterns of virtue were more conspicuous in the past than now, as were the men of high intellectual type and attainment. It must follow, as the average of each succeeding age grows higher, that individual eminence, in anything, becomes less pre-eminent. With this advancing average, the competitions of life become more vigorous, and the spirit of inquiry into individual action more bold and relentless. Moreover, against some particular vicious tendency of the present, we see the corresponding virtue, standing out in the record of the past, and dwell upon it with longing. A single illustration will convey and point my meaning. There is to-day a tendency to extravagant habits of life. We see as we look back that there was, as a general proposition, more simplicity a hundred years ago. By a false generalization we are led to the conclusion, that since a certain degree of simplicity is better than a certain degree of luxury, those days were therefore all better and these days all worse. Simplicity of manner of life is a virtue, therefore those who manifested this simplicity in the past were better than those whom more complex habits bind in the present. But how if that simplicity were mainly the result of narrow means and limited opportunity? Simplicity is not the only test of virtue. Was the man who rode with his wife on a pillion in 1676 because his contracted means forbade a carriage, by this circumstance a better man than he who drove in his rude and cumbrous chaise in 1776, or than he who drives in the commodious, even luxurious, carriage of the present day ? Does a sound logic compel this conclusion from this change of circumstance ? Is there a necessary and logical connection between discomfort and virtue, or does the latter spring from the former as its natural fruit ? Then must we sigh for the hair shirt, or the pillar of St. Simeon Stylites. Is religious profession necessarily more genuine from being austere, uncharitable in its judgments and forbidding in its observances, than when illustrated by the graces and charities ? Is the man who turns the furrow in a secluded corner of the earth necessarily and from that circumstance a better man than he who tends the loom or guides the engine amid the busy hum of cities, coming, in his daily walk, into immediate contact with his fellow-men ?

I suggest these queries, challenging this disposition to consider simplicity of life and its surroundings, in the early days of our country, a sufficient equivalent, and more, for much which makes life admirable to-day, — for far-abounding charities, for sympathies developed and matured by constant and ready intercourse with men, for knowledge broadening and deepening its channels, for high schools and colleges, for the railway, the power loom, the telegraph, for broad and generous views by want of which the simple isolated life is usually marked.

Nor, while denying that enforced simplicity of life is the sum and embodiment of all virtue and excellence, is it necessary to deny that some return towards it might well chasten the spirit of the present day, so abounding in the long results of time, which the Fathers dreamed not of. To such return this centennial year which, as it were by a special Providence, brings with it unexampled commercial disaster and distress, may well admonish the generation of to-day. How easy such a return may be is illustrated by the example of Washington (who maintained at times, and especially during his presidency, a dignity and pomp of state which none of his successors in that office have ventured to imitate). A curious instance of his self-renunciation, which in the narration must cause a smile at the *naiveté* of the commendation, is related by one of his contemporary statesmen. "General Washington has set a fine example of severe economy. He has banished wine from his table, and entertains his friends with rum and water. This is much to the honor of his wisdom, his policy and his patriotism. And this example must be followed by banishing sugar and all imported articles from our families. If necessity should reduce us to a simplicity of dress and diet becoming republicans, it would be a happy and a glorious necessity." A declaration twofold in its significance, illustrating the suggestions I have made as to the simplicity of revolutionary days, and the longings even then entertained for a return to plainer manners.

It is then a false generalization which concludes, while lamenting some particular error of the present from which the past was in great measure free, or all the ways in which the infirmities of human nature work themselves out to-day, that we are, on the whole, degenerate sons, and this illustrated more frequently than in any other way, by the primitive simplicity of manners among the fathers. I claim, on the other hand, joyfully and in veneration of the men who laid the foundations of our civil liberties, that, on the whole, the present days are the best the world has seen; that, on the whole, steady progress has been made in all that develops the better part of human nature, that our country has grown, not only in material resources, but, on the whole, in public virtue, that occasional lapses, and brief eras of lapses, when conspicuous instances of unfaithfulness in public relations and in private trusts have been brought to light, are not to be taken for permanent discouragement, but at most are but the intermittent recessions of a rising tide, that repining for the absence from the public councils or from the seats of judicial learning, of men of as conspicuous talent as those of former days is unwarrantable, since the pre-eminence of individuals is diminished by the higher average of those around them. Probably no one will seriously claim, on reflection, that the aggregate intelligence of any public body, is less now than in earlier days. The difficulty is to make leadership recognized, when surrounded by so much that approaches it in original quality.

Let me show how the greatest public evils, like those of which we complain to-day, were mourned over by one of the purest patriots of the Revolution, as existing throughout that period. We hold up the unfaithfulness of public officers as in painful contrast to the fidelity of those of the revolutionary era. Yet John Adams, in 1776, speaking not in the heat of debate, nor goaded to stern utterance by the rigor of party necessity, but in the quiet confidence of domestic life, said, " We are most unfaithfully served in the post-office, as well as many other offices, civil and military. Unfaithfulness in public stations is deeply criminal. But there is no encouragement to be faithful; neither profit, nor honor, nor applause is acquired by faithfulness. But I know by what. There is too much corruption even in this infant age of our republic. Virtue is not in fashion. Vice is not infamous." Who despairs of disinterestedness in public and private service to-day, and in this regard deplores our national degeneracy? The same illustrious man

3

said in the same year: " The spirit of venality, you mention, is the most dreadful and alarming enemy America has to oppose. It is as rapacious and insatiable as the grave. We are in the '*fæce Romuli, non republica Platonis.*' This predominant avarice will ruin America, if she is ever ruined. If God Almighty does not interfere, by His grace, to control this universal idolatry to the mammon of corruption, we shall be given up to the chastisements of His judgments. I am ashamed of the age I live in." Does the venality of the present day call for sterner rebuke than these words convey ?

And with reference to this very simplicity itself, which is sometimes assumed to be so characteristic of the beginning of the century just now closed, Mr. Adams, commenting on Necker's essay on the true principles of executive power in States, says,

" A man who, like myself, has been many more years than Mr. Necker ever was in the centre of public affairs, and that in a country which has ever boasted of its simplicity, frugality, integrity, public spirit, public virtue, disinterestedness, etc., can judge from his own experience of the activity of private interest, and perceive in what manner the human heart is influenced and soothed by hope. Neglect and sacrifice of personal interests are oftener boasted than practised. The parade, and pomp, and ostentation, and hypocrisy, have been as common in America as in France. When I hear these pretensions set up, I am very apt to say to myself, 'this man deceives himself, or is attempting to deceive me.'"

Not a few good men are grieving to-day over the tendency of a portion of our people to indifference to the preservation of the national faith, as presenting a contrast, in the present time, to the sturdy upholding of it by the Fathers. Yet, on this point, in his day and before the close of the last century, Mr. Adams said : " It is a mortifying circumstance that five months have been wasted on a question whether national faith is binding on a nation. Nothing but the ignorance and inexperience of the people can excuse them. Really we have not a right sense of moral or natural obligation. We have no national pride, no sense of national honor."

Sadly some deplore the increase of government influence and patronage, and the tendency of those in power, at the present day, to press prerogative unduly against the liberties of the people, as well as the dangers of intense party spirit in its influence on the popular mind and conscience ; and in this regard contrast the early days of the republic with our own. Yet this same philosophic statesman, speaking, as before, calmly and in familiar correspondence, said, in language which may find its almost exact application to the circumstances of this hour, —

"I have always thought it injudicious to make any attempt against the governor, knowing, as I do, the habitual attachment to him, as well as the difficulty of uniting the people in another. The consideration he gives to a very profligate party is very pernicious to the public, but he is stimulated, in part, by the opposition to him, and he would not do less out of office. The constitution of our government is calculated to create, excite and support political parties in the States, mixing and crossing alternately with parties in the Federal Government. It will be a perpetual confusion of parties. I fear we do not deserve all the blessings we have within our reach, and that our country must be deformed with divisions, contests, dissensions and civil war, as well as others. * * * May God, of His infinite mercy, grant that some remedy may be found, before it is too late, in the good sense of this people."

Many persons, well-informed in general, strangely forget the plainest truths of history, in their disposition to depreciate the present in comparison with the past. At the time of our great Civil War, nothing was more common than to hear it cited as a proof of our decline in the spirit of patriotic self-sacrifice, that it was necessary to offer pecuniary bounties, in order to induce men to serve in the national army. Yet as early as 1776, Congress offered twenty dollars and a hundred acres of land to every man who would enlist for the war, and in 1778 five hundred dollars were offered by towns in Massachusetts, for recruits for nine months. There was no vice in our late army which did not find its counterpart, in kind if not in degree, in the patriot army of Washington. Then, as later, the sutler preyed upon the soldier, and the hoarse voice of Hook resounded through the patriot camp, with its selfish and discordant cry. The same jealousy among military officers in high command which we have seen so lately exhibited warred against the efficiency of the army, and protracted the exhaustive struggle.

"I am wearied to death," says Mr. Adams, " with the wrangles between military officers, high and low. They quarrel like cats and dogs. They worry one another like mastiffs, scrambling after rank and pay like apes for nuts. I believe there is no one principle which predominates in human nature so much, in every stage of life, from the cradle to the grave, in males and females, old and young, black and white, rich and poor, high and low, as this passion for superiority ; but I never saw it operate with such keenness, ferocity and fury, as among military officers. They will go terrible lengths in their emulation, their envy and revenge, in consequence of it."

I cite these contemporaneous declarations of the highest authority, not in disparagement of the Fathers whom we venerate, but as an encouragement to men of to-day to believe in their times and in themselves, to show by one witness among many, and by one whom all who listen will admit to be entitled to the fullest respect, that the very vices we most deplore among ourselves in public life were deplored not less deeply by those men who, amid all these drawbacks, laid strong and enduring the foundations of our government. Even better than they knew did the Fathers build. For who of them, in the moment of highest prophetic ecstacy, would have dared predict for his country the glory and success it has achieved among the nations of the earth ? If we have not eradicated the vices of those earlier days, we have added to them the triumphs of the present, triumphs of intellect, of personal freedom, of free thought and the advancement of learning ; and I venture to add, also—in view of the severer strain put upon them by the fiercer competitions of the day—of public and private morals. Notwithstanding the recent developments, of defalcations, financial dishonesty, moral delinquency and crime, it may be fairly claimed as a triumph, at least of the negative character, that a gigantic civil war has closed and left behind no greater track of moral ruin. Of civil wars it may well be said, in the language of Burke, " They strike deepest of all into the manners of the people. They vitiate their politics ; they corrupt their morals. They prevent even the natural taste for equality and justice. By teaching us to consider our fellow-citizens in a hostile light the whole body of the nation becomes less dear to us." Unquestionably, the general history of mankind confirms these declarations of Mr. Burke, and, compared with what might reasonably have been expected to follow in pursuance of this rule, our actual experience has been exceptional in the lightness of the evils we have suffered.

A modest scholar, in dwelling upon the disclosures of the past few years, has claimed that " it may be considered one of those epidemics of crime which have frequent parallels in the history of the past, and is not a symptom of incurable national decay and corruption." With peculiar felicity, he cites a similar state of affairs in England in the time of William III., and especially in the years 1694–5. The characteristics of those times have been graphically portrayed by Macaulay's brilliant pen. He says :—

"The peculations and venality by which the official men of that period were in the habit of enriching themselves had excited in the public mind a feeling such as could not but vent itself, sooner or later, in some formidable explosion. But the gains were immediate; the day of retribution was uncertain, and the plunderers of the public were as audacious as ever, when the vengeance long threatened and long delayed suddenly overtook the proudest and most powerful among them. The whole administration was in such a state that it was hardly possible to track one offender without discovering ten others."

Then follows the long catalogue of public crimes and illustrious criminals. All, as in our own case, the temporary recessions of the rising tide of civilization—the rule, progress from century to century ; the recessions of a few years in each century lost in the contemplation of the past. And all this progress but the omen and prophecy of what is yet to come. We stand on this Centennial Day at the opening of a century at the close of which our successors may look back upon us, in the comparison of our attainments in all that makes human life desirable with their own, as barbarians. In the providence of God, in the light of Christianity, in the light also of Science—her younger sister, infinite possibilities of progress are before us. Imagination fails to grasp or define the results of an advance for another century proportionate in any degree to that of this closing one. What truths of nature will not science then have revealed? What arts of life will then obtain, inconceivable now? What shall it now be said will then be impossible? What conditions are to us more inconceivable than were one hundred years ago that power in the expanded drop of water to drive man's iron chariot over land and sea, or that mysterious agency of the skies which, obedient to man's command, gathers with instantaneous grasp the scattered intelligence of the eastern and western worlds and lays it on our table fresh every morning of the year? The impossibilities of to-day fade away then before the unimaginable possibilities of the future. These cannot be defined nor foreshadowed, and the boldest visions shrink from taking shape or form.

> "Vast images in glimmering dawn,
> Half shown are broken and withdrawn."

Their embodiment in attainment through the agency of the restless and aspiring soul and mind of men, our successors here, rests alone with God. Yet, in his Providence, I hold it clear that, bright as is this day of our success and glory as a nation, a country, a race,

these successors of ours, looking back to what we
were, shall descry an infancy of hope rather than
a manhood of attainment ; and, judging us with
charity,—exaggerating, perhaps, our merit as they
contemplate some passing or signal demerit of their
own,—will yet insist that, after all, we were but the
" ancients of the earth, and in the morning of the
times."

I must once more guard against the possible
suggestion that in what I have said earlier in this
address, I design to depreciate or undervalue the
past. Not so ! I would but judge it fairly, and do
justice to the present in the comparison. What I
mean is, that the present shall not be undervalued by
reason of its errors, and to that end I remind you
that our Fathers had to contend with the same evils
in their day, which pressed upon them to the point
of discouragement—at times, even, of despair —
and drove them in their time back to the past for
brighter and purer examples. It is the danger to
which the conservative mind is subjected (and its
judgments are generally to be treated with respect
because its aspirations are generally for virtue), to
feel that all the progress of the present is more
than offset by new and heretofore unexperienced
evils. Is it not true that most of the conventions
and conferences of so-called conservative men and
politicians are marked by expressions of glorifica-

4

tion of the past, in disparagement of the present? Do they not generally exclude its short-comings, its expression of the vanity of human hopes, the exact counterpart it presents to our own trials, from their field of vision? Buoyantly, therefore, and with belief in the present, I remind you that our trials of faith were theirs also, that our hindrances and disappointments were theirs also, and beg you to believe with me that as they overcame we shall overcome also, if we doubt and despair not by the way.

It is appropriate to this Centennial year that its celebration of the National birthday should be marked by considerations and congratulations local in their nature, as well as by those relating to the greatness and glory of our country. The reasons which led to the colonization of this land, so remote from what, in that early day, was known as the Christian world, the considerations which, in the next century, led to the establishment here of a Republic, the National struggle, the National victory, have been in the past and will be to-day, set forth in completeness by orators who, from their more distinguished position, address a field large as the country. And the President of the Republic, reiterating therein the expressed wish of the National Congress, has suggested that the addresses delivered to-day in the various towns of the land, may be, in some degree at least, based on and made to illustrate the local history of those places ; so that they may to some extent, by statement or reference, constitute a permanent addition to the details and materials of the history of the country. No suggestion could be better timed or more truly in accord with the spirit of the day. The history of our country is, in a degree at least, the sum of the histories of its towns and cities. In the usual exercises in honor of the anniversary of the National Independence, the disposition of orators has almost invariably been to dwell upon the aggregate glory of the country, rather than upon the less conspicuous and, it may be confessed, less interesting details of municipal experiences. Yet these illustrate the whole subject, and a knowledge of them is indispensable to a full comprehension of the growth and true grandeur of our institutions. Here are the primal springs of empire. From the town meetings, in communities like this, emanated the influence and declarations which stirred the National conscience, strengthened the National heart and sustained the National arms in the great struggle of the Revolution. And I will show you from the original records of this town, that from its meeting-house went forth lofty utterances in denunciation of the pretensions of the mother country, and in determination to obtain redress of grievances, years before the Declaration of Independence had rung its notes of liberty through the land. In contemplating then the history of our town we turn from maturing results to primary beginnings, from the comprehensive and general to the essential and elementary particular, "*non sectari rivulos, sed petere fontes.*"

Nor should the leading points in the history of a town be suffered to remain unfamiliar to its inhabitants of successive generations. There may be little room for originality or claim to the credit of research and investigation, yet he renders no unimportant service who, by bringing these points anew before the men of to-day, aids in the creation of a familiarity which must animate and inspire. Who first explored that wilderness which now blossoms around us like the rose ? What influence led to that exploration, and laid the foundation of the consequences which followed ? Where was the first house built ? Where was the rude meeting-house, whose walls first listened to the voice of public prayer in this valley ? Who was the first martyr in the great crusade, which ended, though conducted long with varying fortunes, in the triumph of Christianity over Heathenism, and of Civilization over Barbarism here ? In the Providence of God it was ordained that the red man should disappear from our land, and that land be peopled with a new race which should, in the course of time, develop all its wondrous possibilities. What were the relations of this valley to that aboriginal and fated people ? Independence of foreign domination was to be won by blood and sacrifice. What part did the Revolutionary Fathers of this town bear in that heroic and protracted contest ? With what spirit did they meet the onset of imperial power, and with what endurance bear the exhausting strain of long discouragement and deferred hope ? A vast rebellion against the government of our country was to be met and overthrown, and rivers of blood flow, to which those of the Revolution were but mountain rills. How did the sons of our sires rise to this new crisis, and prove from what lineage they sprung ?

You see that these inquiries bring us at once to the contemplation of the springs of National greatness, while the answers which might be truly made to-day (for I shall not attempt to answer all), inspire us with honorable pride which needs no concealment or apology, and kindle anew our attachment for our birthplace. A blessing follows. For as is eloquently and earnestly observed by Southey :—

" Whatsoever strengthens our local attachments is favorable both to individual and national character. Our home—our birth-place—our *native* land : think for awhile what are the virtues which arise out of the feelings connected with these words, and if you have any intellectual eyes, you will then perceive the connection between topography and patriotism. Show me the man who cares no more for one place than another, and I will show you in that person one who loves nothing but himself. Beware of those who are homeless by choice. You have no hold on a human being whose affections are without a tap-root. The laws recognize this truth in the privileges they confer on freeholders, and public opinion acknowledges it also in the confidence which it reposes on those who have what is called a stake in the community."

In cordial compliance, then, with the executive recommendation, I ask you to contemplate with me some of the leading points in the history of our town; its original settlement and the character and purposes of its founders, its early growth, its contests with the natives, at first mild and hospitable, afterwards hostile and determined on the extermination of the white man. Consider, not only here and now, but elsewhere should any suggestions here made be found a worthy basis of reflection, what were the characteristics of its several epochs, from its original settlement to its destruction and temporary abandonment; from its re-settlement up to, and including, the War of the Revolution; from the close of the War of the Revolution up to, and including, the War of the Great Rebellion; three epochs of local history, during which I think we shall agree that patriotism and public virtue grew, that intelligence diffused itself with time, that increasing social order marked all the eras of our history; that, though there have been occasional failures to come up to the high standard of the duty of the hour, there never has been degeneracy, and that this statement finds fullest illustration in the record of honorable resolve and action which closes the story of each of the last two epochs.

Most ancient of the sister townships of this county, honorable as the gentle mother from whose loins of virtue eight daughter municipalities have sprung who now arise and call her blessed, dignified in her age yet wearing it hale and green, rejoicing not in the mere elements of material growth and prosperity, but rejoicing rather in what she has brought into the world, so that instead of illustrating the swarming growth of population within her borders, she has won the proud title of "Mother of Towns," beautiful in the calm repose of natural attraction as when her wondrous charm first revealed itself to the ardent gaze of the adventurous King, who, first of white men, from the neighboring summit, like Balboa "silent upon a peak in Darien" surveyed this lovely valley, our native town bids us welcome to her borders to-day, and invites us to read anew her simple, yet honorable, annals.

And first of all, before entering upon even this brief historic sketch, must full acknowledgment be made of what has been accomplished for the writer or speaker of to-day by the faithful and untiring labors of Willard. His exhaustive research has left little to be discovered by those whose task it is, *non passibus æquis*, to follow him. It was my privilege to know him, and in the years of my own professional study which were the later years of his life of usefulness and honor, to call him my friend. From him I learned to read the lesson of the past, and enjoy its contemplation. Unallured by the sordid from the intellectual, his delight was in historic studies and he found in them a full and rich reward. He loved this town, the home of his early manhood, where he passed happy years of study and practice relieved by the pleasures of historic and antiquarian research. What he has done to perpetuate its history is itself a part of that history. And it is but justice to his memory to make the admission that, in my own researches upon this subject, I have found little which he has not somewhere stated, or to which his memoranda have not given a clue. Unworthy the orator who attempts to arrogate to himself the credit of others' labors, or who, if obliged from the very necessities of the situation to appropriate their results, does not emphatically and unreservedly make all acknowledgment, and pay his cheerful tribute of gratitude.

" *The persons interested in this plantation being most of them poor men, and some of them corrupt in judgment, and others profane, it went on very slowly, so that in two years they had not three houses built, and he whom they had called to be their minister left them for their delays."* Harsh words, if taken in their literal sense, to fall from the lips of the generous and high-souled Winthrop, who judged so kindly, and whose life was the embodiment of almost every Christian and statesmanlike grace; and they were spoken, and not uncharitably, of the men who first undertook the foundation of this plantation of Nashaway, reaching out from the comparative wilderness of Watertown and Cambridge, to grasp possession of an absolute wilderness, never trodden before by the foot of white man, but which their successors, in another century, converted into a garden of bloom and fruit. And I quote this declaration of Winthrop in the outset, as an earnest of my purpose to deal justly with the past in what is to be said of our local history, nor accord it an undue glory from its being far.

But while it is certain that Winthrop would consciously do no injustice to these men, it is fair to claim that his judgment of them might have been colored by his own higher social relations, and by a degree of impatience at their failures. These were not of the highest class of the men who founded Massachusetts. No names like those of Winthrop and Saltonstall and Endicott are found upon the early records of this town, and it was reserved for a succeeding generation to make even one of them illustrious. That they were plain men is obvious. Their callings were humble and obscure. They were no doubt "corrupt in judgment" and "profane," in the sense that they were not connected with the church, and to that sense, I believe, the expressions of Winthrop may be fairly limited. Nor will I claim for them in their settlement of Lancaster any of the exalted purposes which led the men of 1620 or those of 1630, to the remote and barren shore of Massachusetts. Thomas King was the first Englishman, so far as can at this day be discovered, who saw the valley of the Nashaway; and he saw it, judging from subsequent events, rather with the eye of the speculator than of the religious or political enthusiast. The history of the settlement may be concisely set forth. Sholan, the chief of a small and peaceful tribe, ruled in this valley, having his home between the Waushakum lakes. Unembarrassed by that dignity which in riper civilizations becomes a monarch, he was in the habit of making trips to Watertown, carrying his rude merchandise to a market of consumption or distribution. There he met King, who was induced by his representations to visit this valley. Imagination may portray in glowing language, if it will, his feelings and resolves as he gazed upon its beauties. The record only is that he, with his associates, purchased a large tract of land of Sholan, had a deed of it made to himself and them, never came here to reside, though he with others built a trucking-house, relapsed into the obscurity from which history rescues him for the purpose of recognizing him as the original founder of this town, and disappeared in due season from among men.

It is obvious that my present purpose only allows me to pass in rapid review the men or the events of this early day of our municipality. I must remind you of the chief points and characters in our local history, leaving further illustrations to be set forth in notes, should such further illustrations eventually be deemed necessary. For the exact and full details of any of the epochs, or even its signal events, the hour for which I can reasonably ask your attention would not suffice, and I must dwell more particularly upon this occasion on the relations of our fathers here to the great crisis of the Revolution.

The first epoch, then, can only briefly be considered, in respect of the founding and building up of the town as a settlement and a municipality, and of its relations with the aboriginal tribes. As King is entitled to be remembered as its discoverer, Prescott has the higher distinction of being the first of the associates to become a permanent settler. A plain man too, following the unpretending calling of a blacksmith, he had yet strong lines of character and a tenacity of purpose which no considerations of convenience or comfort could shake. His name is associated, through one illustrious descendant, with the highest walks of American literature, and through another with the glories of Bunker Hill. Silently, with no voice of eloquence to be listened to by an earthly eternity of scholars and men of letters, called to no share in the great contests for personal and political independence, honorably, as discharging all his duties here of primitive pioneer, faithfully, as swerving never from his deliberate and chosen purpose, he lived and died in this valley, an example for all generations of his successors here, of true single-hearted manliness.

You see I am speaking of plain men, and the language of eloquent panegyric or stately eulogium has no place here. They were the rude forefathers of this hamlet. Not one of them held a position in church or state which makes his name familiar to later generations, even of those who dwell within the precincts of his valley home. The story of their life and effort here is of the simplest. It was in 1643 that Sholan gave the deed to King and his associates, and the deed was approved by the General Court. King, a real estate speculator after all, sold out his interest to his associates. They signed mutual covenants with each other to begin the plantation within a given time. But none of them came save Prescott, and even his coming was delayed. The effort at settlement in 1644 failed, as recorded by Winthrop. Further effort was made, under the auspices of the General Court, in 1645, but this failed also. The "undertakers" even petitioned the General Court to take in the grant, but that body, impressed with the importance and value of the location, decreed that the plantation should not be destroyed, but rather encouraged, that it should remain in the power of the Court to dispose of the planting and ordering of it, the difficulties being attributed to the fact that the persons engaged in the business were "so few and so unmeet for such a work."

Thus the enterprise feebly struggled on till 1653. Omitting details and names, this is the abstract and brief chronicle of that early time. Ten years of intermittent struggles had however resulted in the establishment of nine families in the town, and the liberty of a township was granted, not by formal act of incorporation, but liberty of a township under certain conditions, to be subsequently enlarged to full liberty of a township according to law, on fulfilment of the conditions.

This "liberty" may be found in an early volume of the Colonial Records. It is curious, as illustrating not only the manner of legislation at that time but the stress laid on Religion and Loyalty as the conditions of the life of a municipality. The Court, among other things, ordered that "a Godly minister be maintained among them, that no evil persons, enemies to the laws of this Commonwealth, in judgment or practice, be admitted as inhabitants, and none to have lots confirmed to them but such as take the oaths of fidelity." Even those who claim that this exclusion for matter of opinion is inconsistent with the ideas of the present day of political and religious toleration will not withhold a meed of respect from that legislative body in Massachusetts which made thus a due regard for the claims of religious faith and political loyalty conditions precedent to a mere municipal existence.

In the first year, 1653, this community, infant-like, only crept. Not entitled to the full liberty of a township, the inhabitants laid out their lots, and made and subscribed their covenant, a code of regulations, quaint and primitive, but looking to the peace and good order of the community. And now the story of their progress is that of the attempt of the infant to reach out for itself, to try to walk, to make up its own judgments as to what course to follow, and then, despairing, turn for solace, support and guidance to the maternal arms. For they could not use that liberty wherewith the General Court had made them free, and in 1657 petitioned for a guardian, frankly admitting that they were unable to manage their own affairs. Their prayer was granted. Commissioners were appointed to arrange their affairs for them. Under their authority, the needful municipal regulations were established, grievances remedied, bridges erected, water power utilized, a ministry established, the boundaries of the town fixed, restrictions limiting the number of inhabitants removed, until in 1663, confident in their strength, self-reliant, and now justified in that confidence, they asked again for liberty of self-government, and were again invested with full township liberties. And now peace prevailed, and a well-ordered community labored together for the common good. The earth yielded a rich harvest to the earnest toiler of the valley. Population began to increase, and a future of prosperity seemed as secure as was the actual achievement of the past.

And yet a more than Assyrian desolation was at hand.

The recent carefully prepared and instructive address delivered within these walls makes it unnecessary to do more than allude to the calamity which befell this town at the close of its first epoch of history. It may be truthfully claimed for our ancestors here, that their policy toward the red man was not aggressive, nor did they provoke by any acts of theirs the storm of war which broke upon them two hundred years ago, and overwhelmed them in its ruins.

Yet the flaming torch of Philip spared not in its avenging career this peaceful settlement, and the ripe fruit of a score of laborious years was blighted in a day. That savage soul made no discrimination in its judgment between communities, if only they were made up of white men. And in a single winter morning this town disappeared from the face of the earth; and thus he made a solitude and called it peace. Peace returned to Massachusetts, six months later, when Philip died, but still the solitude of this valley was unbroken,—a solitude more profound than when King first looked upon it from the Wattaquodoc. Three years passed, and not an inhabitant returned. At length, in 1680, the re-settlement was undertaken—new families came, as well as those who had before formed an attachment here by residence, and the second epoch in our local history was begun.

It was begun in poverty and privation, but resolutely, and this time no man looked back. It was begun, too, on the eve of Indian warfare, and the close of the seventeenth and the first years of the eighteenth century are marked by a succession of incursions and depredations which paralyzed industry and kept even the hope of prosperity in long abeyance. The blood of those early martyrs, Whiting and Gardner, ministers of this church, was shed for their people. Death and captivity, in equal though varying horror, hourly lay in wait, or pursued with stealthy step each movement of that people beyond the walls of their garrisons. The details of their sacrifices are found in Willard. Not till the peace of Utrecht, in 1713, did these horrors cease.

With the establishment of peace, population and wealth again increased, and with them intelligence and influence. In 1721, the people of " the poor distressed town of Worcester " asked the favor of the representative of this town to use his influence in the General Court in their behalf. Harvard was born.—then Bolton, then Leominster. When the war against Spain was declared, in 1739, the men of Lancaster responded with alacrity to the appeal, and their whole quota perished before Jamaica or on the expedition. The men of Lancaster lay in the trenches before Louisburg, and one of her sons commanded a regiment in that memorable siege. Throughout the French war, the town was constantly furnishing material resources and recruits, and it is stated that a large proportion of its able-bodied men were in the field. Lake George, Ticonderoga and Crown Point bore witness to their valor, nor were they wanting in the last crowning hour of trial and victory on the Plains of Abraham.

Note how the successors of those few feeble and

"unmeet" men of our first epoch had grown, before the close of the second, in strength and influence. Yet a greater trial of their courage and determination was at hand. The war of the Revolution, with its mighty possibilities of weal or woe, was before them, to close the second epoch.

I call your attention to the history of this town during the period we have now reached, as disclosed by its record, with satisfaction and pride. You have listened to the grand enunciation of political truths contained in the Declaration of Independence, and your hearts have thrilled anew as you heard once more those noble and familiar words. But their simple grandeur and impressiveness find fit prelude and introduction in the declarations of the inhabitants of this town as I find them set forth in the original records of its town meetings, when the morning of the Revolution was dawning. And in these declarations, antedating by more than three years the Declaration of Independence, you will perceive an aspiration as lofty and purposes as determined, proclaimed by plain men, probably not one of them known beyond the limits of Massachusetts, as were uttered one hundred years ago by Jefferson and Adams.

These brave words of theirs had in them, I think, the significance of an ultimate determination to be independent of a government in which they had no

representation. Few in America had at this early
day contemplated a separation from the mother
country. Even after hostilities had actually begun,
the Continental Congress declared, " We have not
raised armies with the ambitious design of
separating from Great Britain and establishing
independent States." They evince, at all events,
a resolute purpose to obtain a redress of grievances
under the existing government. The relation of
the towns of Massachusetts to the early stages of
the formation of the sentiment for independence
was most intimate. I do not claim that our own
town was exceptional to others, nor was her
determination announced in more absolute terms.
Her declarations serve to illustrate the general
subject, and so set forth her own position at the
time, and that of similar communities throughout
the State. How the towns were brought into
correspondence upon this subject must be briefly
stated, as necessary to an understanding of the
votes and resolutions of Lancaster.

The head and front of the whole movement was
Samuel Adams, years before the sentiment of the
Congress just quoted was announced. Against
the opposition of all his colleagues, he proposed
and carried through his plan of Committees of
Correspondence, to be appointed by meetings in the
towns. Of Adams, Governor Hutchinson wrote

that he was "the first person that openly and in
any public assembly declared for a total independence." Hutchinson denied the right of the towns
to discuss in their meetings public questions of
general interest. The town of Boston, inspired
by Adams, maintained that right, and in town
meeting, in November, 1772, voted :—

"That a Committee of Correspondence be appointed, to consist
of twenty-one persons, to state the rights of the colonists and of
this province in particular, as men, as Christians, and as subjects,
to communicate and publish the same to the several towns in this
province and to the world as the sense of this town, with the
infringements and violations thereof that have been or from time
to time may be made."

The Committee reported to town meeting, setting
forth their rights and grievances. These last form
part of the history of those towns, and are familiar
to all students of that history. The Boston town
meeting voted to make an appeal, by means of
Committees of Correspondence, to all the towns in
the colony, " that the collected wisdom and fortitude
of the whole people might dictate measures for the
rescue of their happy and glorious constitution."

The responses of the towns were unreserved and
emphatic. The spirit of resistance was awakened
throughout the land. Many of these responses are
preserved in the records of the Boston Committee,
and sound the clearest notes of American Liberty.
It would be interesting to quote them here, for the

action of our towns, acting in their distinctly municipal character, in contributing to the formation of a revolutionary sentiment throughout the land has not been so widely understood as it ought, nor so fully appreciated. But the action and resolves of Lancaster are typical of them all.

Judge of the spirit which prevailed here, by this warrant for town meeting, for the first Wednesday of January, 1773:—

"Worcester, ss. To the freeholders and other inhabitants of the town of Lancaster legally qualified to vote in town affairs, Greeting:

In his Majesty's name, you are hereby required to meet at the meeting house in the second precinct in Lancaster, on the first Wednesday of January next, at ten of the clock in the forenoon, then and there to act on the following articles, viz:

1. To choose a moderator for the government of said meeting.

2dly. To take into consideration the Dangerous condition of our Public Affairs, in particular the Independancy of our Superior Judges, and to take such measures as shall be thought proper.

3dly. To choose a Committee to draw up our grievances and Infringements upon our Liberties, and to lay them before the town, when the town shall so order.

4^{thly}. To consider and act upon the request from Boston Committee.

5^{thly}. To give our Representative such Instructions as the Town shall think proper, Relative to our Privileges.

6^{thly}. To choose a Committee to return an answer to Boston Committee and to correspond with any other Committee Relating to our Privilege and to inform the town on their Transactions from time to time.

7^{thly}. To act and do anything that the town shall see proper to withstand the Present Progress of our Enemies in Indeavoring to take away our Priviledges.

Dated at Lancaster, Dec. 22, 1722, and in the thirteenth year of his Majesty's reign."

At the meeting:—

"On the third article, voted to choose a Committee to Draw up our Grievances and the Infringements upon our Liberties and to lay them before the Town when the Town shall so order.

Voted, to choose seven men for the Committee.

Voted, to choose Wm. Dunsmoor, Messrs. John Prescott, Aaron Sawyer, Jonah Kendall, Joseph White, Nathaniel Wyman, Ebenezer Allen.

Voted, to adjourn this meeting to Tuesday, the nineteenth of this instant January, to the meeting house in the first precinct of Lancaster, at ten o'clock, to receive the report of the Committee.

On the adjournment from the first Wednesday of January to Tuesday, the nineteenth of the same, then voted to Receive the above said committee's report.

On the sixth article, voted, that the above Committee be the Committee to make a return to Boston Committee of the proceedings of the town of Lancaster.

On the fifth article, voted to give our Representative Instructions as Followeth:

As you are chosen to represent this town in the general assembly of this Province, we take this opportunity of informing you of our sentiments relative to the unhappy state of our Publick Affairs. You will Perceive by the Resolves which are herewith sent to you, the light in which we view the encroachments made upon our Constitutional Freedom. Particularly you will observe our serious opinion of a Dependancy of the Judges of the Superior Court on the Crown for their support, that they are already so dependant, or that it is in contemplation to make them so. We have great reason to fear also an act passed in the late session of the British Parliment, intituled an act for the better preservation of his Majesties Dock Yards, &c., Does in a most essential manner infringe the rights and Liberties of the Colonies, as it puts it in the power of any wicked tool of administration, either from malice or policy to take any Inhabitant from the Colonies and carry him to Great Britain, there to be tried, which by the expense and long detention from his occupation would be the destruction of almost any man among us, altho his innocence might finally appear in the clearest manner, and further the late commissions for taking persons in our sister colony Rhode Island, and sending them to Great Britain, there to be tried upon suspition of burning his majesties scooner Gaspie, is an invasion of the rights of the Colonies and ought to excite the attention of the whole contenant.

We expect that you will use your utmost efforts this session of our general assembly, to obtain a Radical Redress of our grievances, and we wish you success in your endeavours, and which we cannot but flatter ourselves from the late happy change in the American Department you will meet with. We confide in your ability and firmness in all matters which may come before the General Court, assuring you of the support of this town in all your legal proceedings, and earnestly praying that the Great Governor of the world may Direct and bless you in all your ways."

The Committee at an adjourned meeting, reported the following Resolves and Instructions:—

1. Resolved, that this and every other Town in this Province have an undoubted right to meet together and consult upon all matters interesting to them when and so often as they shall judge fit, and it is more especially their duty so to do when infringement is made on their Civil or Religious Liberty.

2dly. Resolved, that the raising a Revenue in the Colonies without their consent either by themselves or their representatives, is an Infringement of that Right which every freeman has to dispose of his own Property.

3dly. Resolved, that the granting a sallary to his excellency the Governor of this Province out of the Revenue unconstitutionally raised by us is an Innovation of a very alarming Tendancy.

4thly. That it is of the highest importance to the security of Liberty, Life and Property that the Publick Administration of Justice should be Pure and Impartial, and that the judges should be free from every Byass, either in favor of the crown or the subject.

5thly. That the absolute Dependancy of the Judges of the Superior Court of this Province upon the Crown for their support would, if it should ever take place, have the strongest tendancy to Byass the minds of the Judges, and would weaken our confidence in them.

6thly. Resolved, that the extension of the power of the court of vice admiralty to its present enormous proportions is a great grievance and deprives the subject in many instances of that noble privilege of Englishmen, Trials by Juries.

7thly. Resolved, that the Proceedings of this Town be transmitted to the Town of Boston."

I make no apology for producing at length before you these most interesting and original contributions to our local history. It is remarkable that they should never before have seen the light, since they illustrate so fully and effectively the tone and spirit of our fathers.

The warrant for town meeting Sept. 5, 1774, shows still further the current of thought and opinion in the community, soon after the passage of the Boston Port Bill.

The second article is

"To see if the town will do anything towards the relief of the suffering Poor of the town of Boston, occationed by a late act of Parliment, for blocking up the Port of said town or to act or Transact anything relating thereto.

3dly. To see if the town will come into any agreement for non-Importation and non-Exportation of Goods to or from Great Britain, or to act or transact anything relating thereto.

4th. To choose a Committee or Committees to act or do any thing or things that the town shall think proper to be done or acted, by any agreement with any other town or towns in order to get relief in the best and most easy way from our present Difficulty, inflicted on us by the late Act of Parliament, and to act and do any matter or thing that the town shall see needful to be done, and Report to the Town from time to time what they have done, and to receive the Town's orders to act and do what the Town shall think proper to be done and acted. *   *   *

9th. To pass such votes as the Town shall think Propper to be done to get Releaf from those oppressive acts of Parliment which hath been inflicted on us lately, and to act any thing that said Town shall think needful Relating to the Congress and to accept and Ratify what they shall do if sd town thinks fit.

10th. To pass any vote or votes that may be thought needful in order to get Releaf in our present Distressed circumstances, by our just rights and privileges, as we think, being taken from us.

11th. To see if the Town will vote to abide by our Charter Rights and Privileges."

At the meeting it was voted

"To choose a committee of seven persons to be a committee of correspondence for sd county."

And the Committee was chosen accordingly, of which Wm. Dunsmoor was the chairman.

"Voted, that the Committee make report to the Town of their doings from time to time, as expressed in the warrant.

Voted, that any number, even less than a majority of the above committee, shall be sufficient to represent the town as a Committee of Correspondence.

Voted, That the Town will Indemnify the Constable for not returning a list of the Freeholders for Juries, under the late act of Parliament.

Voted, to raise fifty pounds, for to buy ammunition with, to be a town stock."

At an adjournment of this meeting it was further

"2^d. Voted, that there be a hundred men raised as volunteers to be ready at a minute's warning to Turn out upon any emergency, and that they be Formed into two companies and choose their own officers.

3^d. Voted, that the said volunteers shall be reasonably paid by the Town for any services they may do us in defending our Libertys and Privileges.

4th. Voted, that Dr. Wm. Dunsmoor be empowered to enlist 50 men in the old Parish to serve as volunteers.

7

5ᵗⁱ. Voted that Capt. Asa Whitcomb be empowered to enlist 5) men in the second parish to serve as volunteers.

6ᵗⁱ. Voted, to buy one field piece for the use of the town."

At another adjournment, September 28th, it was

"Voted to authorize two field pieces instead of one, and to send one man for the Proposed Provintial Convention to be held at Concord on the second Tuesday of October."

And on December 12, 1774, it was

"Voted, to choose a committee of 3 persons to draw up an Association League and Covenant for non-consumption of goods, &c., for the Inhabitants to sign, and Capt. Gates and Capt. Whitcomb were chosen."

At another adjournment,

"Voted, to buy 5 hundred wt. of ball suitable for the field pieces."

"Voted, to buy 3 hunᵈ wt. of Grape Shot."

On the 31st October, 1774, this town

"Voted to choose a Committee to post up all such Persons as continued to buy, sell, or consume any East India Teas at some Publick Place in Town, and that Doct. Josiah Wilder, Ephraim Sawyer and Aaron Sawyer be a Committee for the above Purpose."

On the 2d January, 1774, it was

"Voted to choose a committee to receive subscriptions and donations for the suffering Poor of the Town of Boston, occasioned by the late Boston Port Bill, and to carry in the donations to some one of the Committee in a fortnight from this day."

Also,

"Voted, to adopt and abide by the spirit and sense of the association of the late Continental Congress held at Philadelphia to choose a committee to see that the said association be kept and observed by the Inhabitants of said Town.

"Voted, that the above committee have no pay, but do the business gratis."

Other votes were passed from time to time, in

accord with the spirit of these. Thus I have allowed these men to describe themselves to you. Ye shall know them by their fruits, for thus they resolved, nor did their resolves fail to find embodiment in action when the time for action came. Their wise prescience foresaw the crisis which must be approaching, and provided means for meeting it with vigor. The morning of the 19th of April, 1775, brought its summons, and the company of minutemen, of which I have cited the formation, was instantly set in motion towards Lexington. The company of horse repaired to Cambridge to assist in checking the anticipated advance of the British into the country. Thus early in the field in defense of that liberty they had resolved must be maintained, our fathers did not cease from their patriotic exertion till liberty was won. Two of them fell at Bunker Hill, the first martyrs of the town in the cause of independence, and few were the regiments of the Continental army from this section of the country, in the ranks of which the men of Lancaster were not found, or in which they did not exercise commands of more or less dignity. Time will not allow me to enumerate them. The names of all the fathers of the town are found on the rolls, and Willard gives a catalogue of not less than ninety-two persons in the service who thus represented the early settlers. Exclusively of Lexington and

Bunker Hill, more than three hundred, all, or nearly all the able bodied men of the town, were in actual service in the field. The town encouraged them by generous bounties, as its records show. There was a delay in the response to one of the later calls which seemed like a momentary faltering. It was in 1780, and a leading patriot of the town declared that response to the call was impossible, as the repeated demands of the country had exhausted the power and resources of the town. But the spirit of sacrifice shrank not finally before this exigency. The men were furnished, liberal bounties were granted them, and they hastened to the field.

I do not think it can be claimed that the town furnished great military leaders, or that any of its citizens held high commands. Yet the names of Whitcomb and Haskell deserve honorable remembrance among the brave heroes of that day. Of Whitcomb a contemporary relates an anecdote which illustrates the true greatness of his character.

[From the *New England Chronicle*, Jan. 11, 1776.]

" Deacon Whitcomb of Lancaster, who was a member of the Assembly of Massachusetts Bay till the present war commenced, had served in former wars, and been in different engagements ; served as a Colonel in the Continental Army, but on account of his age was left out upon the new regulation. His men highly resented it, and declared that they would not list again after their time was out. The Colonel told them he did not doubt there were sufficient reasons for the regulation, and he was satisfied with it ; he never blamed them for their conduct, and said he would enlist as a private. Colonel Brewer heard of it, and offered to resign in favor of Colonel Whitcomb. The whole coming to General Washington's ears, he allowed of Colonel Brewer's resignation in Colonel Whitcomb's favor, appointed the former Barrack-master till he could further promote him, and acquainted the army with the whole affair in general orders. Let antiquity produce a more striking instance of true greatness of soul."

Henry Haskell served honorably as a Colonel, and of Andrew Haskell, a Captain, Willard gives a brief and pleasing sketch, showing him to have been possessed of a spirit of patriotism which rose superior to personal considerations. These were the officers of highest rank who served in the war of the Revolution from this town ; but there were several Lieutenants and subalterns, and their record, as well as that of the enlisted men, seems to have been one of honor.

Meanwhile the spirit of patriotism was maintained at home, and displayed itself occasionally in a striking manner. The town records show that black lists were prepared of persons who used articles of importation, and of persons supposed to be unfriendly to the patriot cause. A committee was appointed to collect evidence against "such persons as shall be deemed to be internal enemies to the State." These names stand upon the records of the town to-day. I will not recite them, but it is worthy of note that the name of the minister of the town is found there, though afterward stricken off, on his earnest protestation that his country had no better friend than he.

I have thus displayed, drawn from original sources,

though with a brevity adapted to the occasion, the record of this town in the war of the Revolution. It is one of devotion and sacrifice, early begun and continued to the end. The articles of confederation and perpetual union between the colonies were accepted by the town in 1778, and the Constitution of the Commonwealth in 1780. The second epoch of our history ended in peace, though in extreme poverty and distress, and the third epoch began.

Almost its first public event illustrates the single step from the sublime to the ridiculous. The General Court granted permission for a lottery, upon the petition of the town, to enable it to raise money to repair its bridges. And the men who in 1773 uttered the lofty resolves and instructions to their Representative which have been read, in 1783 accepted the benefit of the provisions of an act which not only conferred on them powers of folly, but, in the scope of its provisions contemplated penalties of infamy. On the 15th of February, 1783, this act was passed, and was approved by John Hancock, then Governor. The penal section is as follows:—

"And it is also further enacted if any persons shall forge, counterfeit or alter a Ticket any and every person so convicted shall be set on the gallows for the space of one hour with a rope round his neck, or shall pay a fine not exceeding one hundred pounds to the use of the Commonwealth, or shall be imprisoned not exceeding twelve months, or be publicly whipped not exceeding thirty-nine stripes at the discretion of the Justices of the same Court who are also hereby empowered to inflict one or more of the said punishments on such offenders if they see fit.

Feb. 15th, 1783.

In the House the bill having had three several readings passed to be enacted.

TRISTRAM DALTON, Speaker.

IN SENATE, Feb. 15, 1783.

This bill having had two several readings passed to be enacted.

SAMUEL ADAMS, Prest.

Approved.

JOHN HANCOCK."

Surely it is an instance of something like relapse and temporary degeneracy, that from 1782 to 1790 fourteen classes of this lottery were drawn, with a result upon the whole unfavorable to the cause directly in hand, and greatly injurious for the time to the general industry and morals of the community.

Doubtless the temptation was great to resort to any means which promised favorably for meeting a public and exceptional expense. Doubtless this portion of the country was utterly exhausted by the war. Moreover, a sound circulating medium, that indispensable basis of commercial prosperity, was wanting. Yet the lottery consumed instead of adding to the general wealth, and provided a remedy which aggravated, instead of alleviating, the community's disease.

I have left myself no time to dwell upon the

details of the third epoch, and, indeed, my object has been, in great measure, to bring before you the relations of this town to the war of the Revolution. This last epoch also had its alternating scenes of peace and war, though, till towards its close, the presence of the latter was not felt in a degree of severity comparable to that of the Revolution. The causes which led to the rebellion known as Shays' war, in 1786, in which Lancaster played an honorable and patriotic part, are set forth simply and philosophically in the pages of Rev. Mr. Thayer's address. A reasonable number of our citizens joined the forces under General Lincoln, and remained with him to the end of the controversy. In the war of 1812, also, the men of Lancaster were found faithful in arms, and loyally and patiently bore such sacrifices as that war entailed upon them.

It was at the close of this epoch that the crowning proof was given that the spirit of the fathers lived in the sons. Nearly two hundred of our best and bravest, the flower of our youth, went forth from their peaceful homes to defend our liberties on the field of battle, and to die if need be, that the republic might live. The history of the Great Rebellion is yet to be written, and the day has not come for it to be written in the full impartial light which lapsing time throws on past events. It will be a history filled with the story of great battles, and long campaigns, and valor individual and collective such as few histories have disclosed. In that history, we remember with pride to-day, no word can be written which will reflect discredit on any of the sons of Lancaster who marched forth to battle beneath our country's radiant flag. You were the witnesses of the devotion with which they dedicated themselves to that great and holy cause. You saw them press forward to that mighty conflict, not gaily " as to a festival," but earnestly, as to the discharge of the noblest duty of the citizen and the soldier. Your prayers and benedictions followed them. You were witnesses of their departure to the field, and you welcomed back the survivors of that gallant band with tears of grateful joy.

But other tears fell for those who went forth, and returned not when battles were over and victory won. The homes that knew them in their day of youth and bloom, know them no more forever. Yet if to the spirits of the departed is granted some cognizance of what is done in this earthly home of their affection from which they have passed to higher spheres, the knowledge of our gratitude may form a part of their rich and heavenly reward to-day. They died for us, and yonder memorial speaks to us tenderly of the story of their heroic

8

deeds, and tells us how lofty a calling it is to die
that our fellow-men may live, and live not only, but
be free. Nor was it death, but life and immortality
which waited for them and received them, when
they seemed to us to die. For, in the poet's words,
so fitly chosen for inscription on the tablet which
pious gratitude has erected to their memory :—

> " We never can be deathless till we die.
> It is the dead win battles. No, the brave
> Die never. Being deathless they but change
> Their country's vows for more, their country's heart."